For Anne
from Mike
with love &
congratulakes
on your book
soon
health. CM.

Gallery Books
Editor: Peter Fallon

DRAWING BALLERINAS

Medbh McGuckian

DRAWING
BALLERINAS

Gallery Books

Drawing Ballerinas
is first published
simultaneously in paperback
and in a clothbound edition
on 19 July 2001.

The Gallery Press
Loughcrew
Oldcastle
County Meath
Ireland

ISBN 1 85235 291 4 (*paperback*)
    1 85235 292 2 (*clothbound*)

The Gallery Press acknowledges the financial assistance of
An Chomhairle Ealaíon / The Arts Council, Ireland, and
the Arts Council of Northern Ireland.

Contents

for Jamie and Judena Leslie

At Mullaghmore

Earth's memories in the natural dyes
of curtains half-fitted to each other.
There was a deep today
in their different starting-points
as if non-being thought
it had somehow got the better of being.

To love the world of that hour
was to hear the weather-forecast
for a day already lived through
siding with the hurricane
whose presence or absence was the same.

The islands hung together
through the tasteless water.
Though something stayed back
and did the telling
every one of us
was the one who remained.

The Dead are More Alive

As if their eyes could still open,
were resting from their beauty, still
burning very quietly, like candles,
there is something in them that goes beyond
murder, something denied to the eyes,
the eyes being used for movements
denied to the limbs.

Even if you did not see it, nevertheless
it grazed the skin of your mind
with a slashing as if on flesh
by an open knife blade, slicing
everything in two.

A mere fifteen minutes from my room
the sky was still, as though
it would always be this colour.
It spread out, way, way out in the moment
with such wide-open eyes, you
yourself felt viewed.

You were shielded against what you saw
only by never looking away,
you broke down what you saw
by not turning your head,
as one stares at a map so as never
to be outside the world.

Your seeing did not change you,
your eyes grew accustomed
to remaining open, and gathering
the senselessly scattered things.

I avoided reading any items
about them, but I listened to the sounds

of the day stretching across the city,
as if everywhere people expected
bullets to strike again.

The air was a loud nourishment;
it smelled of burnt paper,
it sounded liberated.

I looked for a head as though
to follow its directions,
and the head became very round,
sawing the air, the body broad and rough
as the entire past reaching into later.

I passed four heads in the living-room,
their footsteps lay very far downstream,
though everything was so near, as though
a mountain could be breathed
and this ultimate breath preserved.

The day clashed inside me, till
I felt its blood-filled collapse,
and wanted to tear out from my soil
everything it had planted, then invite
people into my emptiness
where last night's kiss had left
a shell-pink in my cheek,
like a fire laid in readiness for autumn.

The fire that heated them was out,
one red volume pushed out by the next.
But mute as peacocks released
from their vividness, we would not
have been speaking so gladly
about the same thing.

Drawing Ballerinas

We are the focus of storms and scissor-steps.
A young girl that dressed up as a woman
and pulled her gown tight across her breast
now pays men to dance with her, as we would tie
the leaves to the trees and the trees to the forest.

A ringlet of hair tied with black silk
rests in a medallion of white shell, a machine-gun
in its nest, a crease in the middle of a flower.
The hair describes a protecting curve, a repetition
that is a completion, a dip in a mountain.

And the lines' desire is to warp to accommodate
a body, a lost and emptied memory of a lost
body, the virgin mind emptied from or of it,
to discover the architecture of pressed-together
thighs, or lips that half-belong to a face.

The body turns in, restless, on itself,
in a womb of sleep, an image of isolated sleep.
It turns over, reveals opposing versions of itself,
one arm broken abruptly at elbow and wrist,
the other wrenched downwards by the force of the turning.

It settles under its own weight, like some weighty
nude. It flattens to the surface on which it lies,
a series of fluid, looping rhythms, let loose
by one last feeling. As if it had obligingly
arranged its legs, or joined those imprisoning arms.

The oval of the head is a wire folded
in tension to spring back at right angles
across the neck from which it has been lifted.
And what are those unnerving sparks of matter,
the astonishingly open, misaligned eyes?

That suffer like a camera, and fall asleep
a great deal to subdue the disquieting
existence of others — an aerated grey,
but the page stays light, the paper with ease, at ease,
possesses the entirety of the sheets they occupy.

The contours become brittle and start
to fracture, as if the body-burden
with its stripped-down beauty, having rested,
removed her necklace, had put her gown
back on, tied back her hair, resettled her hat.

So that underlaid whiteness is reunified
by light into a breathing white, an undivided
whiteness, a give or take of space
across or within that same whiteness,
that simplest of solutions, the same whiteness everywhere.

'This poem was written to commemorate Ann Frances Owens, schoolfellow
and neighbour, who lost her life in the Abercorn Café explosion, 1972. The
painter, Matisse, when asked how he managed to survive the war artistically,
replied that he spent the worst years 'drawing ballerinas'.

Condition Three

Dawn, that I always thought of as fixed,
the most closed country, embers more often.
Her brokeress womb mosaics a breadth of dusk,
an overnight autumn.
Some deep, unsweetened, sour-smelling ingredient
elbows out the time-related twittering of birds,
nightcrests, walking against pillows.
So that I miss their never-denied noise,
like the largely unheard sounds of war,
the colour of war, and find myself wishing
I were a weather-whipped rocket,
walking into news of any kind.

An unreal warship sculpts the coast
with its watchful, eloquent English,
its cool, watered path, from a midcentury
midwinter to a clockless marriage summer,
has frozen all time but its own.
It has probably hurt someone I knew
or there is some hurt beginning to happen,
its slow bleed bringing eyes
down into pages, mouths down
to the onion-thin sheets of paper
butterflied, ebonied by the bombs.
Its aloneness corners on to mine,
is quilted on, like land.
It spreads open my warrened days
by the dayful, all its seamless miles.

I am listening in black and white
to what speaks to me in blue, in that peacock
power of voice, whose vistas furnish the house
till the night, an enchanted day, overwhelms
any man-made light. When there is a distance
to it, or a fast from the incense of talk,

it is wound in other voices, in mouths sewn
in protest, in arms crossed behind necks
and eyes which are almost too calm.
A sudden set of midsentence years
will be served like some hours,
or the last time your bare lips'
uncertain shrines were used.

The Mickey-Mouse Gas Mask

In the country of comparative peace,
conscious of trees, I taste my far-from-clear
citizenship: like continental mourning kept
in an Italian hurtwood marriage-chest.

I have never been out in so black a night,
people stood in the roped-off streets
watching the sky.
The Clubhouse's pretty double drawing-room
had gone completely flat, its back
as if a giant knife had cut it through.
Huge blocks of stone were thrown up in the air
like cricket balls, furnishings were flung
fifty yards on to the course. Every window
missing, the church had only its spire left.

This war of movement seems to travel
like a reverse letter 'L', the long arm
loaded with Maid-of-Honour cakes. The other
a dog-photographer's water-only meal.

A Ballet Called Culloden

It was a painted journey,
their mountains were a week by fast horse.

I bent my body to the climb,
bringing it from its order of march
into its order of battle,

and blew on the slow-matches of my fingers
to give them skill.

My saddle-housing gave off gentle
light across the spine of the moor
where the broad road passed over
the graves caught in its mouth,

each holding aloft a flaming
pine-knot of five bows,
heather, gale, ling, oak and myrtle.

The ground rose at seventy-five
paces to the minute, and a black roof
of hats bared their primrose facings
firing at the words of the psalm.

So the day was conceived in its commonness,
a well-known green, and the answer
to my floral question was allowed
to fall straight down

till the trees that were needed
for other men, or eight-oared boats,
found that flower reeling in his fluted hand.

Act of Settlement

He carried Ireland around with him
like the cardboard tongue pinned to their backs
or the outline of a handgun
photographed in his jacket.

His hands that alone seemed made for it
were so full of America, when they begin
the arrangement as if it had been
but this day thought of,

it will probably be some strange
patchwork, a basket
of shot, sap-green eggs,
hitting a building with peaches

like an open blossom with the insides
of fruit stringing its stem.
And the graces of government
that I meant to bring to my own lips,

as well loved in those rooms
as in kitchens of clay,
those prancing letters could bring it all
back with a whistle,

my impanelled friend, diverting us
with another rebellion, during the blush
of this, invisible dyke, still keeping the ship
up for the benefit of the turnpike.

Martyrdom-de-Luxe

With one English shoe
and a black glove over
his duelling hand
each time he received communion,

it was only in English-coloured words
his name was, or ever could be,
changed by language-washing
to being nearly Saxonized

by a rain of dukes
in Warwickshire. At Calais
he had thrown, with an oceanic feeling,
his protective tricolour cockade

defiantly into the shared water
untouched by oceans
of his sister island.
The harbour crept about

the trapped Atlantic
until the water's bone-cleaned
lacework was lost to sight
and he was just like feathers in my hand.

Wood being, wood martin,
in the day-darkness of the unconscious woods,
I doubt if his iron ration could be heard
in the clearing six yards off.

Not even the joyous banshees
in their songs from the faces

of the high rocks know
who will live in his cage in the future.

He breathed the *De Profundis*
tilting out from the wall
as though it were his pretended
agreement to no definite heaven,

while in our secret Englands
about twenty minutes past four by the Dublin clocks
we sat down like galley-slaves
in a gravemate's calm.

The Moses Room

I who have eyed the weather constantly
and wanted to call the sea back from its bed
am nobody's host and nobody's guest, in the
all-white snowclad living-room, in the curve
created by the road. The road is an invert,
a woman, the bachelor wind blows the colours
of the haphazard sailing-boats before her,
and I feel compelled to follow it to the end,
for R's sake, though it still rushes backwards
and forwards between the same two places;
still with the Englishness of a railway,
or a thin line of gold braid edging
the predominantly silver canal of my desire.

A rain picture is the picture of the year,
with two pianos back to back, an inscription
over the fireplace saying 'Two lovers
built this house'. And the gossip of all the girls
who danced there was the man who lunched
with me in London, who wore silver
where a diplomat wears gold. Like a swarm
of bees let loose upon visitors, he suddenly
swept the flowers off the table, as if
a secret wasp had sawn at his finger,
the only entry in my 'Who's Who'
not carried forward into 'Who was Who',
unseaworthy, more my lover than he knew.

You who have changed the name
of your third son, with four underlinings
and two different pens, because his name
meant a sum paid by a bridegroom
for a bride, reverse the name of 'Kingstown'.
The horses are wearing frost shoes
for the home-stretch, after three round trips

they became recusant, rough in their play:
the blot of rust mould discolouring his letter
like a leap-second salutes when the guns say.

Oration

for Harper Daniel

You, command in the changing light,
are shedding your leaves, the oldest of them,
the oldest disciple: you know our martyrs.

As if one has just smashed something unearned,
everything takes place as if after your death,
the whole sea breaking up that comes each time,

its rhymes buried in folds of meaning
wrenched into a small space, the line engraved
around the mouth between the actor

and the crowd. You, ideal book
that contains the world, you question
born of unsatisfactory answers

and promise of a new question, not dreamt
upon but excavated, as dying,
the lilac drinks the watching world.

So its after-death is also a before-death
impossible to cross by will or grace.
You shattered, you surrounded by flowers,

that unheard-of number Shakespeare names,
fit unmoored the measure of the sky
not like that lifeless stone, the moon,

prisoner of its calling and unflagging charm,
but the Boyne salmon prized in its bend
in water colour, never out of season,

its great eye redemptive in the weight
of its dry lustre. How it returns
hedging to its Virgilian setting

its motion heavy with rest,
and how I am forced by sound alone to learn
from that afflicting language

with its busy words, never to use
a word that has not first been won,
nor write your name till it becomes the man.

Monody for Aghas

You won't be a voice to me any more,
the weather of my own creation
repeating the highest possible shared
symptoms of the day. You were born

in a leap year, just as one day
was ending and the next beginning,
in a new time zone where landscape
has become language . . . blue bloom

of the faultless month of May,
with its heart set on conquering
every green glen . . . springtime
in action, springtime unfolding

into words, a literature of spring,
spring in place, time and eternity,
she-bird in its velvet dress
of soft blackbird colour,

maroon seed dashed from the hand.
Let me taste the whole of it,
my favourite tomb, the barbarity
and vividness of the route,

my due feet standing all night
in the sea of your pale goldfish
skin without body, its glimmering
sponged out by a tall white storm:

the red flag could not have made you
less Irish, your once-red lips before
and after folded together and left down
quietly, never to be parted,

that were forced open, strapped open,
by a sort of meal of a fixed gag,
a three-foot tube previously
used on ten others,

dipped in hot water, and withdrawn
and inserted, clogged and withdrawn,
and cleansed . . . your broad heart
became broader as you opened

to the Bridewell and the Curragh,
Mountjoy and Ship Street.
It was fifty hours without
plank bed or covering

while Max Green, Sir Arthur Chance,
Dr Lowe and the JP
almost wept, then attended
a banquet, before you smashed

the cell window for want of air,
and the Sisters of Charity
at the Mater Hospital
painted your mouth with brandy:

like a high-mettled horse,
soothing and coaxing him
with a sieve of provender in one hand
and a bridle in the other,

ready to slip it over his head
while he is snuffling at the food.
Today the fairest wreath is an inscape
mixed of strength and grace —

the ash tree trim above your grave.

Black Raven on Cream-coloured Background

'A sparrow hawk proud did hold in wicked jail
Music's sweet chorister, the nightingale . . .'
— Anon, written for Thomas Weelkes, from *Hesiod*

I too was sorry that he was not shot,
really not thinking of it as quite possible
either, the rainbow lifted off the ground
and gathered into a turquoise ring —
I'll ground myself in its radiance.

Tired is not what I am, but I think
I really did know him, having seven
years to study him, still, he was different
every day. He was already a generation
old — a generation more, our paths would converge.

But he had to be given up for lost
so we would be a little scared
all the time by the unloved government,
its small excoriations, its semi-lunar
depressions, its bells tied up and muffled.

And his heartsounds were not among us
for years, in any way the world
knows how to speak, his body and tang
abloom with tapers quenched,
his soft-collared, slightly uncomfortable smile.

Though it would take a ship
to hold all the messages, I only half-read
by hearsay all the other names
of the fields; how finishing his last field,
he then cut all the flowers in bloom

in the school garden. The allied fields
kept tryst with the grass being cut
from under my fingers by bullets.
He had invented a lamp with his last
look at the earth, to send the first leaf on,

walled in by himself, and fit for idling,
fit for restraint in handcuffs, waist belt,
muffs or jacket in splints. They said
the bonniest, most dashing of fighters,
his pistol in the ivy at the back of an old shed.

The Muse takes care of it, deeply recessed,
so primitively crushed: she holds
and freshens in this air of withering sweetness,
close-knit and somewhat stifling, the barest shadow
of its most stately, most mobile mouth.

Angelus Bells and the Light Glinting in Her Hair

A searchlight swung across the lake
like a marriage subject to season.
All the ungrown tissue of its sucking depth,
its sharp green, less and less to be found.

The long narrow lane of his face
filled his turned-up hood, as if
a few jags of unpainted bushes
could become a tempest picture now.

War spirit, mirror in the uniform of a wheel —
let us become strangers again.

The Truciler

The bullet cleared the briars
off the top of the ditch, drove
particles of his bone at a four
miles per hour walk, to rejoin a road
like a swine with a tusk
which has grown round into the head.

Within minutes of that noontide,
priceless manuscripts floated over
the city, releasing the scent
of partition, and the stray light
in the straitjacket of the Republic
paid out the head money of his soul.

Now the dwelling house is always
locked, the sound of horses in a nearby
stable pipes through the fighting.

Corner boy in excelsis, with towels
framed all around the railings,
Ireland is yours: take it.

Hazel Lavery, The Green Coat, 1926

Agreed image, of your open self, your personhood,
do not put me into a sadness like your own,
though I am using your heated body with its
easy mark of beauty, its narrow grip on a segment
of the abstract world, for some clues.

He has been able to bring your inner sun
to full view, a real heartbeat and a lucid mind
inhabiting a body degrading into matter:
like a rosary made of plum stones, built
en colombage, your hospitality towards death

is the light of my own country. The lamp
without oil in your spine a hand-made candle
to light me to bed. Your sense of chastity
starts a shape in me attached to life at all
four corners, saying what your beauty means to you.

A wave heaping itself to feast like a plant
on much of what flames in my eyes, the world
of speech, a world that seems bared of its covering,
and has not a bone in its body. You are walking
within a tulip, and a fire of sea-coal in your house

not yet numbered leaves a blue path through
the warm cinder of your head. You throw a veil
of sinewy deception, of half-grown leaves,
over your eyes, walking up Air Street that moon-
ark body you had so often laid down . . .

so that the living seem to go to bed
with the dead, most seasonably, a boy hobbles
with a log at his foot to kiss the bell-handle
of your lodgings: his most used words inking
that wintry mantle of aged snow, floating

in the middle of the unstitched page. You have
what used to be called a military bearing,
which is that of a child asleep on a cross,
the whitish patina of verdigris and rose
carmethian that begging soldiers forge

on the eight hanging days, as their ivory ticket
to the damaged sky where heaven tries to see itself.
And it is as though you actually wore armour,
with nineteen horses killed under you, seated upon clouds,
your seas unsailed since his blood fell directly

into the unfixed horizon.

Moonflowers

Your small-paned colander window
no longer fights the many-windowed sunlight.
Autumn's manoeuvres almost detribalised us,
a few bells rang out of tune
in the vote-giving city,
some cheering from recruits
will never be called upon,
flags hanging flaccid
in the November damp.

Constables had only recently replaced
the old-fashioned watchmen,
but neither peace nor war would satisfy them.
My dream of a month ago
is like iron-collared poured water,
double arches of water then under snow,
the scene that went before that sleep.

If a final omen were sought
by so mild and open a winter,
the hearse-like clouds
are things which are passing away.
Peace has defeated
the careless arrangement
of his slack hands.
And spring is still awaited
by the ornamental trees in the ossuary,
by the English roses added to our gardens,
by that war-worn figure,
standing in the firelit room,
asking for his wife:

by the moonflowers at the edge of war,
their hardest buds the studs
in our shirts.

Red Trial

I wanted to buy a man made from sleep:
an underground man, a new glittering iceberg.
But his perilous eight-ninths was so over-alive,
when I tried to interview the ever-present dead,
I wanted the truth and all I got was his body.

Close-lipped and stern, a mere husk, in convict
clothing; with an air of looking back on a love-
affair; actor with a single line, framing sentences,
sitting tensely forward in a pistol-point of time,
so all you could kiss was his fingertips.

A letter addressed would almost certainly reach
his half-an-hour away, H-for-Henry, Tudor-shaped
end house: whose invisible fourth wall was
the whole world watching — a keyhole to which
an eye of every age was pasted.

The radio, that fair-faced conspirator, purred
with a positive belongingness, whispered
his name in Irish, wished to touch him where
a bill of dark particulars, black with one white
glove, hung like an act in the living-room.

'The defendant must have flown during a redundant
winter, when no planes landed, to a burned-down hotel.'
As if last January were standing floodlit, after
a long detention on mere suspicion, free to be silent,
entitled to a hearing, on an autumn day in court;

while sour soldiers, overgrown boys, met summer
half-way in their fall ensemble. What he had 'done'
had a winter-smell of mice and old wood;
its enormity dazed me like a sunburst, marking
his inmost bloom with a blunt malice

to a pirate flower curiously streaked,
though it is the hand holding it that is cracked
and seamed, by its power to harbour him —
the sea in labour every fifteen minutes
against what it should host, the all-night diver.

Crumlin Road Courthouse

Where my house touches the church
its restful surface is exalted
by an enchanted wall.

If dark spires would melt away
rather than having to be blown apart,
if a cloud could change

the flowery essence of its shape,
I could divine the river,
the hospital, the citadel,

and listen to some phantom rocks
just showing beyond the rim,
protected by the lifelike water,

growing in the ravishing sea
like a shell — life-giving ghosts
mirroring nothing.

In every language it is already
past midnight; all they give us
in the way of sunlight is a log

veiled by the fire it feeds,
arrows starting from a half-sketched
armful of snow shorn of its forest.

At night to enroll your love, my breast
in secretly alert sleep
falls blemished into my hand,

walking without my new heart
on this fated and only island,
and counting the steps of the sun.

Oh waste of moon, moon that sets
unused, waste of spring lilac
in claiming such a burning word

for me alone. What suppleness
there is in the shadows
of the least landscape,

the clear blue rectangle
of the long window, the sumptuous thunder
of the sky and river festivals

the vase gave birth to.

Saxon Slave Clock

By ear instead of eye,
the time can be found in the dark,
the hour marks and hour lines
countersunk in the wheel.

A shadow falling on a flight of steps
in the neighbourhood of noon
is not perfectly sharp,
though walls flare and toss,

and the odd window of thin horn
burns with selected colour.
At a pre-set hour,
a self-going clock, being wound,

releases a light arm
carrying a jewel
on plain, uncut brass,
a pierced ruby as a bearing

distributing the new, marine hours
for the position of a ship at sea.
On the shortest winter afternoons,
or the shortest mornings,

the hands of clocks exposed
to the free wind and high weather
count the light
of the mean, imaginary sun

like an ink trace
on a smoke surface,
quarter-chiming its celestial
equator, or the age of the moon.

At the outer end of spring,
the arc of their swing,
that was equal to the hours
during the major part

and near the mid-point
of the order of the day,
dies away closely.
It's the watchman's tell-

tale clock, driven inwards
by the four tides of a given star,
that's the ideal timekeeper,
night dial in a wood lantern.

Gaeltacht na Fuiseoige

New Year's Day, 1997

Cubes of sky-wielded silence
yellow the light: the light
that would be glad
to bathe itself in you.

When for years I have months
and my soul chimes
like an inhabited word,
a thinking which sucks

its substance, barer now,
enticing meaning, laying
word against word
like pairs of people,

broods in the wound,
an admitted infection,
the highroad's central
greatest ought.

43

The Swan Trap

I wrote to winter to remain
watchful, in second place.
When a word was wanted
I drowned myself in moonlight.

The dazzle-painting of my inner bone
and underskin went on burning.
My wings locked in the rich prolonged
red of the dead water.

But the wing which is the sail
is tamer than it was — slow-flowing
conversation is now as fast as silk:
railroad songs can put back the trains.

Like upright script my neck's outstretched
pillow creases take off into the wind:
like a hint of sea on the air, a gentle blue,
a blue feather pattern quivers

the much decorated, swiftest part of the river.
And so intensely the proper inhabitants
of the true wild dive together,
their killable gold-plated shoulders

diving deep, into each other's
wilder places, where an ancient enemy
or an evaporating memory
concentrates on a square-lipped

lasting peace, superbly green,
its heart as large as a bull,
its arteries wide enough
for a child to crawl through.

A Perfume Called 'My Own'

When a spider makes the initial move
from one side of a lane to the other
she leaves, but she does not leave.
Her ingrained life erupts within her,
she crawls along the bidden thread
she has created, recluse about town,
holding on to herself like utter fragrance,
like a warm but ordinary woman
whose bones float about her body,
whose clothes just cover her breasts.

How strange it was that you should have been
that person, so near to the earth,
weaving in and out of my life, where everything
was missing, by a hedged path,
where to walk in a wood was to be fired at.
The lost summers continued incognita through
the long emotional autumn tunnels
till January showed no sign of returning
and September passed to the clear month
of June, merely by changing the ribbon.

The face of morning reflected
in the lid of a piano has a smudged
mouth; the inside of a week
of dark, almost black, daylight
drinks thirstily the bloom from your head
like the snow-clad scent of an orange tree.
In a room full of half-dead flowers and fruit
winter's petal-like discovery is your Napoleonic coat:
whose English is English, whose shoulder blades mean
how the twenty-four hours go round.

A Mantra of Submission

My miniature shore is a lick of gold
iced over as his singing dated head.

From the caged area of the garden
he murmurs across newly-found pillows
furring my single-hearted arteries.

At midnight, like a storm that feels
my presence,
twelve raw Muse-grapes
free me from all the years of blame

of being ill-at-ease among pacifists,
war-harnessed as a soldier to his voice.

The Pochade Box

My gold child has a soldier's head.
There are touches of flesh on her black-
bordered silver coat, she is armed like spring
for one hard day with a citron wing.

Her youth scents the framing room
though she looks suddenly old,
like an old warhorse seeing out the season,
her bitter and subtle mouth never at rest.

Air from the morning kisses her on her hair;
winter wears on in a fluid, creamy
frost that has a skin, the essence
of the day allows no newness

but a new way of eyeing the city.
Nearly half a life of bad weeks
leaning on the arm of anyone
who would grab hold of your hands

closes a door behind her, in a language
of pauses quickening to a snap.
Announcements of freshness from the tin
sky mislead and taste her blood.

Like two moonlights falling correctly,
she paints the large white roses into the dark
of her absolute childhood, she treats
the taffeta flowers as her key:

not just to twilight but the purple
of the floral night, the weather-tinted street
of air in the centre of whose upper edge
she skirts low and playfully sails away.

The Colony Room

If you are touching, you are also being touched:
if I place my hands in prayer, palm to palm,
I give your hands new meaning, your left hand calm.

You define my body with the centre of your hand;
I hear through the shingled roof of your skin
your ear-shaped body enter the curved floor-line
of my skin. My hands just skim the cushioned opening,
the glitter of your mouth; all woods, roots and flowers
scent and stretch the map that covers your body.

Less touchable than the birth or continuation
of Ireland, in its railed enclosure, your root-note,
in its sexual climate, your kingdom-come eyes,
year-long, inactive lover, durable as paradise.

Like small shocks in the winter, neck to neck,
the mirrors reflected the coloured ray
the evenings needed most, when the day . . .
asked for night in that mistletoe way.

To the Silhouette of a Camel

Treasuring the extinct world of old obediences
that were in my blood, I blessed
with a Franciscan soul the most memorial bird,
but with my soul's flesh drove my still young
heroine into the shell of its name.

If it is a moment of aiming,
bring then, like some dry light, actually forecast
in the raised velvet of time
douceur de vivre, a French river
to these so deeply English shores;

to this not-too-successful rose garden,
where the unheeded chrysanthemums are coming along,
bring a crimson hurricane, a May,
so the sunned-over too-short days
will have a way of being jubilant.

More will be done than the best
of your other doing — as if a voice not your own
were blown in an afternoon untaught
that we could go on trusting until we thought
we were returning to the world.

The Miniver

Another black date, black gondolas
absorbing the blue, trying to renew
our appetite for war like half-a-cake
eaten by a catfish, or a coconut
carved into a fool's head.

Even the most war-weary marauders
at the hour the century was born
were timing Christmas by the light
on their swords, galloping in every ceiling
into the ceiling of a cooler sky.

It was the hand of God at its purest
set the weapons cabinet with its fine holes
deep into the English brown and green earth
of the very lagoon, making use of heaven
to bind His blues with His own ultramarine.

And fettered Mars, so women looked away
from him as black stone, the colour of their thoughts,
so wine flowed from the statue
of sleep-inducing Mercury, a whole raft
of meanings on the inside of their lids.

This brittle peace, a palmsbreadth in length,
is always morning, has that morning glitter,
gives the ever-narrower interior a feeling
of being outside, lines the walls with leather,
crushes the marble floor with her floss petticoat.

She is hope's brother, though the two people
inside her add up to less than a whole:
she is so placid, clean and fresh,
the rhythms of her warrior father invade other colours
than the lilac of her vase-room flesh.

Copperheads

I think 'firelight' and I call the dream
new eye, brushed ankle, dazzling voice,
speech that sounds like speaking,
from the bone-cup of his tongue's root.

The muscles of his long language upswing,
uncommon touch the half-learned language
in my eyes. They train my eyes to live
behind bars, and then to see again

how war itself became lovelier,
long-necked, clove-eyed, with a widow's
walk, travelling passionately from summer
to winter with the terrible velocity

of Demeter. Became more needed
not because he is not there
but because he is. Icy nights
that spiced the killing time

mull the wrenching day.
Our hurried eyes and death-encrusted
mouths long for the first land sound
in the dance of war, a hoarse wind

thinly patriotic, warming and softening
and sharpening that red rim angled
up into petals. Sun-rotted,
she has gardened him, his blowing gold

from black soil, the high yellow
flower of the army in a space
that seemed free of the dead,
in their earth-cloaks and over-essence.

Stark blue, the snow ticks,
shaking the sadness out,
shortening the endless home-
away-from-home war by trying

to regroup, not turning back.
In the northernmost marketplace
they smear grease on the guns
and seal the shells in jugs

like their right to choose the war,
saying, will we have to defend
our re-knowledge of their country
when the tide slopes brown, in one lifetime?

The Disinterment

Too much snow, too fast,
on two of the loveliest rainclad
autumn nights, your planned,
yet not perfected, absence.

Deep-quivering Muse, army-dissolver,
you who have driven war away,
dance with me, anoint
my warlike eyes with peace.

Taste the bottle containing
the thirty-year truce,
the magic wine of the victory-defeat
speaks in your mouth: 'Go wherever you wish.'

My neighbour too was at his window,
his terracotta sunflowers divided
the room by gender, wings of an orphan
auburn bird through his fernery

touched too little his parlour palm.
How hard it is to recover peace
from the arms-dealer by whom
she has been buried!

In the text of peace
the strong argument has hands,
the weak a cloak, but no names
are heard at all.

Our cupping-glasses are filled,
the sky is an oven lying round us.
Backstage of the cavern
of the goddess Peace

stands the belatedly imprisoned
maiden Reconciliation,
untouchable, immobile,
close to her spokesman Hermes.

Why is your thigh-smoke
changing colour, what is this
lustral tear that falls?
Come here or, rather, come into the sky:

where any movement of Peace's head
that cloud-woman, island-woman,
will introduce the aerial, invisible
failed clouds pulling on her ropes.

Closed Eye Song

Silky peace, perfect police,
being both police and crime,
he came with the calm of a cycle
like a quick April, like a season
to fill the basic season of my life.

Not being in any way inside him
while having him inside, I shall
lend him my body, the use
of my stylized heartbeat. Let him
bathe one in the blood of the other.

My neck to him, my shoes
empty of their feet. Let him
touch my number, let me feel him
feeling nothing, one of those kissed
who does not pass the kisses on.

Not to be splashed with sunlight,
his left iris decomposes the gleam.
His solar beauty harpoons me
like a landlocked ship, our milk
house is a cube of solitude.

A fourth of his vocabulary
is this delicious pardon,
his grief-stricken 'not evens'
are smoothly ingested
by the half-seduced night.

In extreme close-up I search
his entire readerly face.
He respects me as the flame queen,
the couple that I was —

scarecrows robbed
of their cross-belts,
and the supple
fabric of their coats.

The Flora of Mercury

In the room there is no Christ
but the goal of vision where my eyes
wander step by step.
Youthful time has bidden him
though he seems immune to time.
Like sunlight in the leaden
recesses of the city,
his open-sided U
has the principal role.
The blue isosceles of his tactile
glance is a Phoenician ship
that knows the sea's pathways
and has followed the same
and only path from the start.

To study a man from his shadow
is to contemplate him banished
from the earth, each part
of his languid, ivory body
perfect and apart,
equal in its freedom.
The peace-wagers exist
in his copied light, a species
of hired corpses, with immovable
horizons, immured
in their waxen secrets.

His rigid gaze shoots
straight ahead, the central ray
of his eye drains the world.
He arrests the servile orbit
of his look, which ceases to behave
like a hand bruising itself against
the initial and deepest layer
of these peace-war paradoxes.

Silence or indifference,
like a domestic muse,
masks the best of war
in the same fabric that makes
that distant, disembodied cloud;
and all this sky touches is free.

After the Honeysuckle

If a man had to watch his own backbone opening
and, nearing sleep, was far enough into heaven
to wear its rim away by slowly kissing it:

the days that he would lose would be cut from the flags,
and the last shot of the war would be beaten shut
like a beachfront road into which night is about

to fully come. The weather mixes its clear numbers,
bringing back to it what must have changed
in me, living upon the strained sun

and now, hand full of leaves, watching it rain,
that old touch, the notes of twilight that have been
in one world and are trying to return to another.

A Waiting Plate

Two island-wide words for life —
our innermost time like a princess asleep
in a rock, and the time-pencil
yellowing the field, charring the sand,
surprising the faultless dawn
with a soundless fever.

Then the road that was like a harp
raising its cheek to the wind
like a sail suddenly unties itself
into an arrow of his or her birthwood
that hurts more than the deep places
of lips, the back of the throat.

The summer floor heavy with sea-shells
veined by the winter door falling open
lets it evolve into a wave
like a slammed door, sealing in
the margins of the day, the taste
of next year's wine in a body kept young.

The sea-line looks at its own hands
stained with sea-damp, slowly copying
its mildness, splashing shadows everywhere
on rosy stones and special earth.
The salt mixed with soft dust has the unearthly
fidelity of the bone of the head.

At the wine-impregnated hour
when wingbeats curse into the moonlight,
the moon a brown grape late and high
puts her mid-heaven lips to the centre of the cobweb,
so pieces of solid air like compressed petals
promise their rooms to her expected kiss.

The Orange Island

It was not the fault of the day
that it held objects fiercely
like a rose cast in brick
from a seven-sister rose bush:
the pivot of the summer
was so full of weather
the curtain of grapes
could barely stretch an octave,
one couldn't count the grapes
on the clear heart of the curtains.

Each storm subsiding
in the gabled looking-glass
spun like a bomb worth
boasting about into unsuspected
freedom.

Every dialect
that danced on his tongue
dissolved her internal dream
of immortality with a kiss.

And part of the prayer was wearing
a green branch like a tinge of sex.
Riverside, near no road, it flecked
and slotted, and felt the handle
turned very softly from the other side.

Jesus of the Evening

We were alone, rebreathing our own air.
Non-lovers. Too much married. Our language
changed to a slowly enlarging interface,
I said it aloud and precious after you.

Unblemished as a warrior at war,
your eyes were dead — no spear-play
climbed or crawled or flowed
with its untiring scarab fire.

Like an old town which clambers over
an extreme tip of land, not a rose-
coloured city winter-ruled, the bud
of our consciousness scented rosaries.

Our strange catechism came to us
unadorned, I brewed your name away,
till heaven fed it, fortunate, important,
embracing the true anti-love of earth.

Butcher's Table

Canary Wharf.

We flew between two sheets of heavenly blue
which crossed the top of the world.
Bank notes fluttered on pavements, and in cool,
arched rooms, eyes matched conversations.

He played me a little sad Chopin, the blue-
out was bright, but the fields were a strange
sour green. At some indefinable signal
a hundred horses moved as one, storks in migration

landed on power cables and burned in blue flames.
Some of the tallest are the shortest now,
the burn cases lie so still, beyond forgiveness,
dark marks show how deep the water rose.

Once again we are alone in the war,
we have torn the skin off rooms like dolls' houses,
we have sown the cemetery with mines, a jigsaw
of bodies mulls the dust. If Overlord has started

you must make the gun part of your arm, squeeze it
like an orange in your palm, write with it as a prayer-
like pencil. But what a little life the dead tanks can take,
as they repair our country, with my gun arm against
    the door.

The Frost Fair

A sudden sunburst, then a world of torment.

The moon, that connoisseur of death,
slept to a miracle, lilac over black,
and left town early on Saturday.

Small, one-eyed town,
downstairs to her satin-stitch,
to a little fixed pain, a continual
motion of the head . . .

She is still lying there,
her face covered with newspapers,
eyes, fingers, here, there, everywhere,

and she might think 'I'
as she did now,
pulling out the leaves
from the birch trees of Birkenau,

all over, from top to toe,
from left to right, longitudinally,
perpendicularly, diagonally,
like twenty ounces of blood
from the body of a superior bird

whose shrine is hanging by its heels
from the shaft of a petrol station
where fifteen hostages were painted
all along the iron.

The Marital We

I can find no simile to fit the shell
of my lover Hope; there are kinds of newspatterns
I can't ask for.

The palm telephone
with its great loops of persuasion
never rang, even to see,
having walked out after the first act,
how it ended, raggedly,
and then return to the beginning.

The feminine form of the unloving adjective
to the masculine noun cannot be heard
in the sterile spoken word, *mariage
blanc.*

But a man can help a woman to loosen
her three-quarter length coat
and put her kept-down head
down beside him, to be lied to,
by old kisses new as cold churches.

From Grace Church to Calvary Church
the dust-edited thin-voiced children
stencilled lotus leaves on slices of years
as in some restless complicated advertisement.

October snow has overloaded your winter,
ruined by the first sprig of old woman's flower:

she sketched a sailing ship and wrote
'Him' above it, a mere muse, low-skied,
to the room.

Manteo

To return to the kiss —
kisser and kissed —
the source of brown feathers
I swallow till it is down:

even a spark to light a pipe
will not leave my premises.

Word-for-word I count
the days marooned by illness
as in a chapel-village
over two unbridged rivers.
The prow of the mountain
mirroring the behaviour
of the absent one,

something organic hidden
on my land, like a blue stone
wrapped in a petticoat,

or the silver-as-moon
inside-of-cloud
stranded shells I bathed with
by summer daylight
reliable as bones.

Lamped lovemonger,
sleeping among your guardian bookcases,
your dreams will be word-films
in the meaning of the night
as love helps a woman
to conceive.

I called your glossy soul,
turning in its unique sunlight
to read the world,
as a ploughman is called
from his plough
to wound a body backwards
and forwards in a stronger way.

My heaven-bent
slumber-pin
the charm-setter bedded
in your body's deepest secret,

the vein that leads directly
to the heart.

It was faultily made
as Christ, my playboy
of saintliness, the noteless
ring glitter

of my lovely, lost leaf
fluttering province
rattling the scarlet ashes
of its judgement wine.

Manteo (*manta,* Spanish for blanket) refers to a procedure to deal with a difficult birth as described by Angela Bourke in *The Burning of Bridget Cleary* (2000).